The Hurricane Story

The last Hurricane
delivered to the RAF
(LF363) was handed over
in January 1944.

The Hurricane Story

Peter R. March

Sutton Publishing

Also in this series:

The Concorde Story
The Spitfire Story
The Vulcan Story
The Red Arrows Story
The Harrier Story
The Dam Busters Story

First published in the United Kingdom in 2007 by
Sutton Publishing, an imprint of NPI Media Group Limited
Cirencester Road · Chalford · Stroud · Gloucestershire · GL6 8PE

Copyright © Peter R. March, 2007

British Library Cataloguing in Publication Data
A catalogue for this book is available from the British Library.

ISBN 978-0-7509-4453-3

➤
*Hurricanes painted to
represent aircraft of a
Polish squadron for the
1968 Battle of Britain
film.* (via M.J.F. Bowyer)

Typeset in 9.5/14.5pt Syntax.
Typesetting and origination by
NPI Media Group Limited.
Printed and bound in England.

CONTENTS

The story of the Hurricane's design and development by Sydney Camm from his successful Hawker biplane fighter series is far less familiar than that of R.J. Mitchell's Spitfire. Yet, as this account shows, the Hurricane probably made a bigger impact on the ultimate course of the Second World War during its first year than the Spitfire. I would therefore like to draw particular attention to the tremendous contribution that Sydney Camm (later Sir Sydney) made to the design of British fighter aircraft for three decades, through to the Hawker Hunter.

I am very grateful to Brian Strickland for the research that he has done into the background and service life of the Hawker Hurricane. Unlike some other famous aircraft with a straightforward record, the Hurricane's story takes you all over the world through a complex web of role changes, conversions and operational use. I would also like to thank Ray Polidano, Director of the Malta Aviation Museum, and Peter Vacher for their kind help.

➤
The Last of the Many.

Michael Bowyer and Derek James have been particularly generous in supplying photographs from their extensive collections. It has been a difficult task to source quality photographs to illustrate the Hurricane's story, since much of its service was overseas in the Second World War. However, I am grateful to the following photographers and collectors, who searched their photo files for me to find suitable historic black and white, and contemporary colour photographs: Kev Baxter, Gary Brown, Sue J. Bushell, Bill Bushell, Richard J. Caruana, Frederick Galea, Darren Harbar, Howard Heeley, Godfrey Mangion, Andrew March, Daniel March, Frank B. Mormillo, Col Pope, Kev Storer, Brian Strickland, Richard L. Ward and Tim Wright.

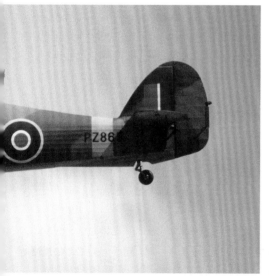

Photo credits
Photographs Peter R. March/PRM Aviation Collection unless otherwise credited.

The Hurricane fighter began its evolution in 1933, when Sydney Camm, the then chief designer of Hawker Aircraft Limited, examined the idea of a high-performance, monoplane interceptor to replace the RAF's Fury biplane. He realised that the only way to increase fighter performance was to move from the established two-wing to a single-wing configuration. In the early 1930s there was still a general distrust of the monoplane among the military, that was rooted back in the structural failures of military aircraft since the earliest days of flying.

It is a piece of cake, I could even teach you to fly it in half an hour.

'George' Bulman, Hawker's chief test pilot, to designer Sydney Camm on landing the prototype after the first flight

Hawker's new fighter was eventually produced to meet Air Ministry Specification F.36/34. The prototype, K5083, made its first flight on 6 November 1935, in the hands of chief test pilot Gp Capt P.W.S. 'George' Bulman. The aircraft was put into production in 1936, three months before the official order, and the first Hurricane I flew on 12 October 1937. Although the Hurricane's performance in 1937 was probably superior to the Luftwaffe's Messerschmitt Bf 109, by 1940 it was already falling behind the Bf 109E. This did not deter the RAF pilots, who proved that with appropriate tactics they could outperform the Luftwaffe in the critical months of 1940.

With its hump-backed appearance and powerful Rolls-Royce Merlin engine, the Hurricane will be particularly remembered

Prototype Hurricane
K5083 seen at
Brooklands, Surrey,
before its first flight in
November 1935. It has
the Watts two-bladed
wooden propeller, wheel-
door D-flaps, tailplane
strut and short radiator.
(via Derek James)

for its key role in the Battle of Britain, during which it equipped a total of thirty-two RAF squadrons. Hurricanes destroyed more Luftwaffe aircraft during the summer of 1940 than the RAF's Spitfires and ground defences together. It served operationally on every day throughout hostilities, in every operational theatre and in many roles.

Well over 14,000 Hurricanes were built (the exact number is somewhere between 14,230 and 14,670), the last being delivered from the Langley factory in September 1944. Hurricanes served on seventeen different battlefronts, including the British Isles, France, North Africa, Sicily, Italy, the Middle East, the Far East and Russia, in the Battles of the Atlantic and the Mediterranean, in Malta and with the northern convoys. During its service career it operated as a fighter, a fighter-bomber, a ground-attack, rocket-firing fighter, a 'tank-buster', a catapult-launched and carrier-borne fighter. Hurricanes bore the brunt of the early aerial fighting during the first three years of the war until Spitfires became available in quantity. They also took part in some of the earliest fighter sweeps over Europe in 1940 and 1941. In October 1941 it became the RAF's first home-based fighter to carry bombs in action.

In 1944–45, with rocket projectiles, the Hurricane was used to great effect against enemy shipping in the Adriatic, and as a fighter-bomber it served with distinction in Burma. Although no longer in production when the Second World War ended, the Hurricane was still in service as a front-line aircraft.

Sydney Camm persuaded the Air Ministry that his private-venture aircraft, initially known as the 'Fury Monoplane', was worthy of official sponsorship. In fact the Air Ministry wrote Specification F.36/34 around Camm's initial design. Utilising Hawker's well-established structural principles, the prototype was constructed of rigidly braced steel and light-alloy tubing with fabric skinning.

The famous Hawker fuselage, which had featured in all Hart variants and the Furies, was retained in preference to the then more advanced metal monocoque fuselage. The aircraft combined the well-proven tubular-metal, cross-braced, fabric-covered 'Warren' fuselage with a new fabric-covered, cantilever, twin-spar wing with 'Warren' girder interspan structure. This was in order to speed production.

◄

The fuselage shape of the Hawker Hart/Fury/Hind biplane series is similar to the Hurricane's, as illustrated by The Shuttleworth Collection's Sea Hurricane and Hind.

The enclosed cockpit was situated over the wing, with a sliding canopy with quick release for emergency exit and a further escape panel in the side of the fuselage between the upper longerons and the canopy.

HAWKER'S HURRICANE

Camm's monoplane fighter was officially named 'Hurricane' in June 1936. It became the first of a new generation of monoplane fighters, destined to replace the two-gun biplane. Broadly resembling the Fury, it featured a new wing with flaps, an inwards-retracting undercarriage and an enclosed cockpit. Sydney Camm quickly developed his monoplane into an effective fighter, completing the transformation from early-thirties biplane, with fabric-covered wings and little protection for the pilot, to metal stressed-skin wings, armour plating, bulletproof windscreen and self-sealing

Prototype K5083 with modified cockpit canopy, retractable tailwheel (unique to the prototype) and tailplane struts. (via Sue J. Bushell)

Early production Hurricane I L1648, which flew with No. 85 Squadron at RAF Debden in 1938.

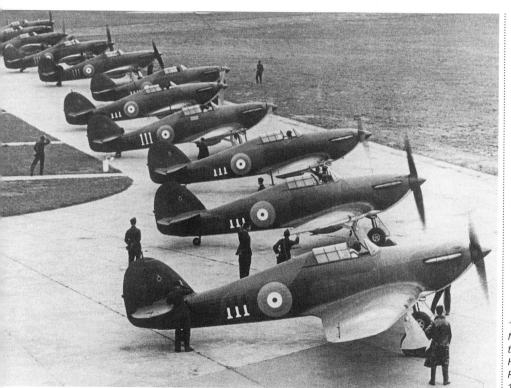

No. 111 Squadron was the first to receive Hurricane Is, seen here at RAF Northolt early in 1939. (via R.L. Ward)

tanks. The undercarriage, with wide-spaced legs and wheels, gave good stability on the ground. The cockpit canopy was mounted relatively high providing good visibility for the pilot. One of the new Rolls-Royce PV.12 engines (later named Merlin), providing 1,030hp (768kW), was chosen to power the Hurricane. Initially driving a fixed-pitch, two-blade wooden propeller, it enabled a maximum speed of 318mph to be reached at 16,250ft. The uprated Merlin III that began flight-testing in January 1939 had a constant-speed, three-blade propeller and became standard on the Hurricane I. An initial contract for 600 aircraft was placed on 20 July 1936 and increased to 1,000 the following year.

The Hurricane's armament comprised four pairs of machine guns, carried in the wings and firing outside of the propeller arc. The American Colt Browning machine gun was chosen and adapted to take the existing rifle-calibre bullet of 0.303in. This version was selected as it was a known quantity and had proved to be very reliable, with few stoppage problems. A total of 300 rounds of ammunition per gun was carried, giving 14 seconds of continuous fire.

In 1937 the Minister for Co-ordination of Defence, Sir Thomas Inskip, persuaded his Cabinet colleagues that a realistic aerial defence against German bombers was possible – this being contrary to popular belief at that time. He managed to divert some of the very tight resources into the production of fighters, instead of the preferred bomber option that had been inherited from the 'Trenchard era'. One immediate advantage was that fighters

Did You Know?
At the time of the Munich crisis in September 1938, Hurricane production had accelerated sufficiently to re-equip a new squadron every month. By the end of 1938, more than 300 aircraft had been delivered from Hawkers.

No. 501 (RAuxAF) Squadron Hurricane L2029, which came to grief at RAF Tangmere late in 1939. Unusually it displayed the commanding officer's pennant prominently on the tail. (via R.L. Ward)

Did You Know?

RAF squadrons began receiving the Hurricane I in 1937, and by the outbreak of the Second World War on 3 September 1939, nineteen Fighter Command squadrons were equipped with it.

were cheaper and could be produced more quickly than bombers. Nevertheless, from 1937–9, 2.3 bombers were built to each fighter produced. Prime Minister Stanley Baldwin said: 'The bomber will always get through.' As a result, bomber development continued to win priority over the new fighters.

Only five RAF squadrons were equipped with Hurricanes by early 1938. The first of these, No. 111 Squadron at RAF Northolt, received its aircraft in January that year. By the end of 1938, the German Air Force front-line strength was more than 3,000 against the RAF's total of 2,000. The Luftwaffe also had the advantage of recent combat experience, as it had been involved in the Spanish Civil War. At that time, Fighter Command reserves were only expected to last two weeks at the most in a war situation. Also at the same time only 10 per cent of reserve pilots were ready for front-line service.

By 1939, the Hurricane was fitted with a de Havilland Hydromatic (licence-built Hamilton Standard) or Rotol (a company formed by Rolls-Royce and the Bristol Aeroplane Company) constant-speed propeller and ejector exhausts. A reflector gun sight was another important addition soon after the Hurricane had its first combat experience in the Second World War.

Hurricane pilots relaxing in the summer of 1940. (via Dr Alfred Price)

At the outbreak of the war, Hurricanes were chosen to accompany the RAF bomber squadrons sent to France with the Allied Expeditionary Force (AEF), where they received their 'baptism of fire'. They equipped Nos 1 and 73 Squadrons of the Advanced Air Striking Force and Nos 85 and 87 Squadrons of the Air Component. The first enemy aircraft shot down by RAF pilots, a Dornier Do 17, was destroyed by Hurricane L1842 of No. 1 Squadron, on 30 October 1939. During the days of the 'Phoney War', a Hurricane pilot from No. 1 Squadron in France, Flg Off E.J. 'Cobber' Kain, a New Zealander, became the first RAF pilot to earn public acclaim with his fourteen victories.

Some of the Hurricanes serving in France during the winter of 1939–40 were of the original type with wooden propellers and fabric-covered wings. As the Hurricane outline resembled the French Dewoitine D.520 operated by the Armée de l'Air, the RAF fighters were painted with distinctive fin stripes.

In the abortive Norwegian campaign of May 1940, Hurricanes of No. 46 Squadron

These Hurricanes from No. 87 Squadron were sent to defend France at the outbreak of war as part of the Allied Expeditionary Force. (via M.J.F. Bowyer)

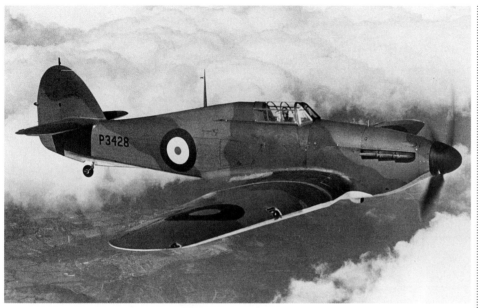

P3428 was an early production Hurricane I built at the Brooklands factory. (via Sue J. Bushell)

were taken into action by the carrier HMS *Glorious*. With the Gloster Gladiators of No. 263 Squadron, they were the only fighters tasked with the air defence of the northern port of Narvik. At this time there were plans to fit a Hurricane with Blackburn

◀◀

From the early winter of 1939–40, RAF Hurricane Is were given red/white/blue fin stripes.

◀

This Canadian Hurricane XII, 5624, fitted with 12-gun wings, was equipped with an experimental ski undercarriage.
(via Sue J. Bushell)

Did You Know?

Because there seemed no prospect of increasing the speed of the Hurricane, on 12 December 1939 the Air Staff recommended that development should be phased out.

Roc seaplane floats but, although flight tests were scheduled for June 1940, the campaign came to an end and the project was cancelled. Plans to fit a ski under-carriage were also abandoned in this country, although a trial installation was later carried out in Canada.

When the Battle of France began in May 1940, German bombers attacked twenty-one Allied airfields. No. 87 Squadron, with its Hurricanes put up fierce resistance. In one day, ninety Luftwaffe aircraft were shot down for the loss of twenty RAF fighters. A further thirty-two Hurricanes were sent to France, but ACM Sir Hugh Dowding, C-in-C Fighter Command, doggedly resisted sending more. A total of 200 Hurricanes were lost in France (about seventy-five to enemy action) by the end of May. Unfortunately many had to be destroyed on the ground to save them falling into German hands during the evacuation.

On 3 June 1940, in the thick of the Battle for Dunkirk, Hurricanes were sent from England to defend the British Expeditionary Force (BEF) and cover the evacuation from the beaches. Some sixteen Hurricane squadrons were in action at any one time. A total of 32 fighter squadrons, 25 of which were equipped with Hurricanes, saw combat over the Channel ports, from which 477 aircraft were lost, including 300 Hurricanes. After Dunkirk, there were only 367 Hurricanes and Spitfires remaining for the defence of Britain.

I must therefore request that as a matter of urgency the Air Ministry will consider what level of strength is to be left to Fighter Command for the defence of this country, and will assure me that when this level is reached, not one fighter will be sent across the Channel however urgent and insistent the appeals for help may be.

ACM Sir Hugh Dowding, Fighter Command's founding commander-in-chief and architect of the Battle of Britain victory in 1940

Although it had been at the forefront of the air war over France, the Hurricane really won its spurs during the Battle of Britain. Its task was the most important of its operational career, confirming that Sydney Camm's design had excellent qualities as a fighter, despite some shortcomings in performance.

In the Battle of Britain, the Hurricane I accounted for more enemy aircraft than any other type of aircraft, and altogether in the first year Hurricane squadrons accounted for more than 1,500 confirmed Luftwaffe aircraft shot down. This was almost half the total of enemy aircraft destroyed by the RAF in that period.

Fighter Command's average Hurricane strength between 10 July and 31 October 1940, the period officially recognised as the Battle of Britain, was 1,326, compared with 957 Spitfires, making it the RAF's principal fighter. There were thirty-two Hurricane squadrons in Fighter Command during the Battle, compared with nineteen equipped with Spitfires.

A total of forty-six Hurricanes had been lost by 31 July. On 8 August, fifteen Hurricanes were shot down, an attrition

Hurricane I N2359, one of the last to be built with fabric-covered wings, was flown by Plt Off L.W. Stevens of No. 17 Squadron at RAF Debden in August 1940 at the height of the Battle of Britain. (via M.J.F. Bowyer)

➤
A formation of nine Hurricane Is during the Battle of Britain in 1940. (via R.L. Ward)

Did You Know?

With a top speed of 335mph, the Hurricane I was slower than its Luftwaffe counterpart, the Messerschmitt Bf 109E, but it was very effective in attacking and destroying bombers during the Battle of Britain.

Two late production Hurricane Is of No. 501 (RAuxAF) Squadron scramble from RAF Hawkinge on 15 August 1940 to intercept an enemy formation. Both of these aircraft were lost in heavy fighting later that day. (via Brian Strickland)

Did You Know?
During the war a number of Hurricanes were 'sponsored' by individuals, organisations, cities and even counties.

rate that posed serious problems for the RAF. Without the backing from the Civilian Repair Organisation, the RAF would have quickly run out of aircraft. On 16 August 1940, Hurricane pilot Flt Lt J.B. Nicolson of No. 249 Squadron earned the first, and only, Victoria Cross awarded to an airman of Fighter Command during the war. He

shot down a Messerschmitt Bf 110 over Southampton after being badly wounded and with his own aircraft in flames. Nicolson then abandoned his Hurricane and parachuted to safety. He recovered from his injuries and later reached the rank of wing commander, but died in 1944 when the Liberator in which he was flying disappeared over the Indian Ocean.

The climax of the battle was reached on 15 September 1940, today commemorated as Battle of Britain Day, when the Luftwaffe's last major offensive was launched, and repelled by RAF fighters.

Famous RAF pilots whose tallies of air combat victories during the Battle of Britain were gained while flying Hurricanes included Sqn Ldr R.R. 'Bob' Stanford Tuck of No. 257 Squadron, the Czech pilot Sgt J. Frantisek of No. 303 Squadron (the top-scoring pilot during the Battle, with seventeen victories), Sgt J.H. 'Ginger' Lacey and the legendary legless pilot Sqn Ldr Douglas R.S. Bader of No. 242 Squadron. Three of the five squadrons of the Duxford Wing, including No. 242 Squadron commanded by Bader, were equipped with Hurricanes. Duxford was a sector station in No. 12 Group, Fighter Command during the Battle and gave its name to the 'Duxford Wing' which inflicted heavy losses on the massive German formations that attacked London at the peak of the battle, on 15 September 1940.

By the end of the Battle of Britain, 695 Hurricanes had been lost, while 1,537 Luftwaffe aircraft had been shot down, two-thirds by Hurricanes. The aircraft themselves were of various standards.

Hurricane painted with the code letters of No. 1 Squadron, RCAF, later No. 401 Squadron, as Mk I P3069, which was flown throughout the Battle of Britain from Middle Wallop, Croydon and Northolt. (Graham Finch)

Did You Know?

Top-scoring Hurricane pilots in the Battle of Britain were Sgt J.H. 'Ginger' Lacey and Flt Lt A.A. McKellar, each of whom shot down eighteen Luftwaffe aircraft.

20

The Luftwaffe attempted to overwhelm the RAF fighter defences on 13 August 1940. No. 601 (RAuxAF) Squadron was among the defending units scoring victories and helping minimise damage to airfields in southern England. (via M.J.F. Bowyer)

Delivered new to No. 605 (RAuxAF) Squadron, Hurricane I R4118 flew forty-nine combat sorties from Croydon during the Battle of Britain.

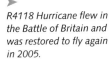

R4118 Hurricane flew in the Battle of Britain and was restored to fly again in 2005.

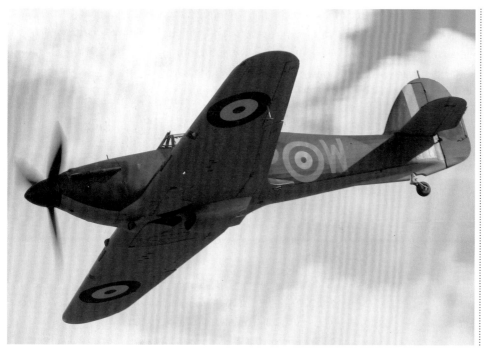

Did You Know?

By the time the famous legless pilot Sqn Ldr Douglas Bader was shot down on 9 August 1941, he had downed twenty-two enemy aircraft and shared in the destruction of four others.

23

The Hurricane destroyed more enemy aircraft in the Battle of Britain than all other British fighters and defences combined. It went on to be developed into multiple roles and fought on more fronts in more countries, and in more theatres, than any other fighter aircraft.

Of the 870 'new' Hurricanes delivered to the RAF during the Battle of Britain, there were forty-nine Mk II Series 1s, while the remainder were Mk Is variously modified. Although the basic top speed of the Mk I was 310mph (498km/h) the engine boost was lifted from 6.5lb to 12lb, which gave a 25mph increase in speed for short periods.

My reaction to my first flight in the Hurricane after the Spitfire was not good. She seemed like a flying bomb, a great lumbering stallion. But, after a few minutes I found the Hurricane's virtues. She was solid as a rock and was a wonderful gun platform. Somehow she gave the pilot terrific confidence. You felt entirely safe in this plane.

Sqn Ldr R.R. 'Bob' Stanford Tuck, who commanded No. 257 Squadron with Hurricanes during the Battle of Britain

NIGHT FIGHTING

The Luftwaffe's switch from day to night attacks in late 1940 caught the RAF ill prepared. There were only twelve squadrons of night fighters in November 1940 and few had the very early forms of Airborne Interception (AI) radar. The Hurricane was not designed for night fighting, but with very little additional equipment installed, a coat of matt black paint, the fitting of anti-glare strips between the exhaust stubs to protect the the pilot's night vision, it made an important contribution.

During the Blitz on England in the winter of 1940/41, Hurricanes flew as night

◄
Hurricanes of No. 257 (Burma) Squadron, one of the units that went on after the Battle of Britain to night-fighter duties, were based at RAF Coltishall for much of 1941. (via R.L. Ward)

Hurricane night fighters had modified exhaust stubs to protect the pilot's night vision from glare. (Howard Heeley)

Did You Know?
Between 1 July and
15 October 1940,
1,994 Hurricanes saw
service with Fighter
Command, of which
523 were written off
during combat flying.
The number of
operational sorties flown
was around 35,000.

fighters in support of Bristol Blenheim IFs and Boulton Paul Defiants. They remained the mainstay of Fighter Command's night intruder and home defence squadrons until the arrival of the Bristol Beaufighter.

Squadrons operating in this role were Nos 1, 3, 43, 73, 85, 87, 96, 111, 151, 245, 247, 253 and 257. On the night of 10/11 May 1941, when the Luftwaffe made one of its heaviest raids on London, Hurricanes

This Hurricane IIC of No. 87 Squadron is painted to represent the CO's aircraft in late 1941.

Did You Know?

Typical sorties flown in the Battle of Britain lasted about eighty minutes but the Hurricane's Browning 0.303 guns provided only 15 seconds of fire power.

from No. 1 Squadron shot down seven Heinkel He 111s and one Junkers Ju 88. These Hurricanes had exhaust flame shields just forward of the windscreen for night operations and no windscreen mirrors were fitted. Landing lights were also installed in the leading edge of the outer wings.

During enemy night raids in 1940, the ineffectiveness of Britain's night defences was a serious problem. Before the use of Airborne Interception (AI) became wide-spread Nos 1 and 43 Squadrons were involved in 'Turbinlite' operations. Power-ful miniature searchlights mounted in twin-engined aircraft, notably Douglas Havocs of No. 1460 Flight, were intended to illuminate enemy raiders so that accompanying Hurricanes could close in for the kill. Hundreds of flying hours were spent in fruitless patrols and exercises before the scheme was abandoned in January 1943.

Did You Know?
By August 1940, a total of 2,309 Hurricanes had been delivered to the RAF (as opposed to 1,400 Spitfires) and 32 squadrons were so equipped, as against 19 with Spitfires.

◄
No. 3 (RCAF) Squadron with cannon-armed Mk IICs was based at RAF Hunsdon in the autumn of 1941 for night fighter and ground attack duties. (via M.J.F. Bowyer)

Malta was at first deemed undefendable, because of its close proximity to Axis-occupied territory, so little effort was made to put the island on a wartime footing until it was almost too late. In March 1940, just two months before Italy declared war, twelve Gloster Sea Gladiators that had been held in store at Kalafrana for use as replacements for HMS *Glorious* were handed over to the RAF to provide a fighter flight at Hal Far. Four were initially erected, quickly followed by another two, while the other six provided spares.

So when Malta was attacked from the air on 11 June 1940, three Gladiators took off from Hal Far to harass the incoming bombers. Because only three aircraft would take to the air at any one time, these three eventually acquired the names *Faith*, *Hope* and *Charity*.

At that time, Hurricanes had started to filter through France to Alexandria, and eight landed at Malta in June. Three Hurricanes departed for Mersa Matruh, leaving five to battle on alongside the Gladiators. The first Hurricane fell in the

➤

Two of the first Hurricanes to arrive in Malta in 1940. Although the aircraft in the background is 'tropicalised', it retains the black-painted underside. (Richard J. Caruana Archives)

Did You Know?

At a critical time in the defence of Malta in November 1940, eight of twelve Hurricanes flown from HMS *Argus* to bolster No. 261 Squadron ran out of fuel before reaching the island and were lost at sea.

defence of the island on 13 July, when, after a long dogfight with Italian Fiat CR42s, Flt Lt Peter Keeble in Hurricane P2623 crashed and was killed. He was quickly followed by a CR42 that crashed within 100yd of his Hurricane.

Despite the urgent need for Hurricanes at home in Fighter Command, there was a pressing requirement to strengthen British forces in the Mediterranean and Middle East. On 2 August 1940 twelve Hurricanes were flown off from the aircraft carrier

◄

Hurricanes on board an aircraft carrier in the Mediterranean waiting to take off for Malta. (via Frederick Galea)

Aircraft and hangars were destroyed in frequent Luftwaffe raids on Malta's airfields. (via Frederick Galea)

With hangars reduced to heaps of twisted steel, most of the servicing had to take place out of doors – as with Z2982 of No. 185 Squadron at Ta' Qali. (Richard J. Caruana Archives)

In May 1941 strafing Messerschmitt Bf 109s destroyed a significant number of Hurricanes at Ta' Qali. (via Frederick Galea)

HMS *Argus* and, guided by two Blackburn Skuas, they winged their way to Malta. There they immediately joined the hard-pressed Sea Gladiators in the vital defence of the island. Operation *Hurry* was the first of twelve such deliveries that eventually supplied 330 Hurricanes to Malta, with a further sixty flying in from Gambut, Libya or by sea in crates.

Their task was also to help to cut off Axis supplies going to North Africa. The first aircraft were initially designated No. 418 Flight but they soon became No. 261 Squadron. A second delivery was planned but unfortunately only four of the twelve Hurricanes reached the island, the remainder having to ditch in the sea. They had been flown off the carrier too far from Malta and ran out of fuel before reaching their destination.

On 4 September 1940 Hurricanes scored their first success against Italian Ju 87 Stukas and six days later Hurricanes of No. 274 Squadron shot down two Italian SM.71s. It was not until December 1940 that the situation really changed for the worse, when the Luftwaffe arrived in Sicily. In January 1941 the damaged carrier HMS *Illustrious* limped into Grand Harbour and

Pilot running to a bombed-up Hurricane IIB at Hal Far, with RN groundcrew turning its propeller ready for starting. (via Frederick Galea)

The arrival of Hurricanes, like this No. 185 Squadron Mk IIC, BW826, relieved some of the pressure on the older, ageing aircraft prior to their replacement by Spitfires. (Richard J. Caruana Archives)

Furious despatched twenty-four improved Mk IIs. These were followed by 160 Hurricanes by the end of June, although many of them went on to North Africa. Three new Hurricane squadrons, Nos 126, 185 and 249, were formed at Ta' Qali. On 25 May 1941, No. 249 suffered a particularly heavy loss, when Messerschmitt Bf 109s of 7/JG26 hit ten Hurricanes during a strafing raid while the RAF pilots were strapped in their seats at readiness.

By October 1941, Malta's Hurricanes were taking the war to the enemy by performing fighter-bomber sorties against targets in Sicily. A Malta Night Fighter Unit was also formed with twelve Hurricanes at Ta' Qali. Flying at night and guided by ground searchlights, they achieved very good results and the enemy raids decreased considerably. By the end of the year, the

became a prime target for enemy attacks. During the following days, attacks on Malta increased in ferocity and Hurricanes were sent to intercept Ju 87s and Ju 88s.

A serious attempt to reinforce Malta's dwindling Hurricane force came in April 1941, when HMS *Ark Royal* and HMS

Did You Know?

Despite the official preference for Spitfire development, the Hurricane had a major advantage – the relative ease with which its thicker section wings could accept a variety of weapons, not least the 20mm cannon.

Hurricane was becoming outclassed, outrun and outgunned by most of the aircraft that the enemy was the throwing into the Malta battle, particularly the Messerschmitt Bf 109F/Trop.

Hurricanes battled on without help from Spitfires until 10 March 1942. During the period June 1940 to July 1942, a total of 87 Hurricane pilots were killed while between 230 and 250 enemy aircraft were destroyed, with at least 115 'possibles'. Hurricanes were finally withdrawn from front-line operations on Malta in May 1942.

SECOND GENERATION PLUS

The Hurricane II, first flown in June 1940, had the more powerful Rolls-Royce Merlin XX of 1,185hp (883kW), with a two-stage supercharger. Few major changes were needed to the airframe, apart from the engine mounting. There were slight alterations to the wings to cater for increased armament, together with strengthening of the fuselage and landing gear to take care of the increased power and weight.

On take-off, power is applied smoothly to full throttle, giving some 3,000rpm and +6.25lb/in² (p.s.i) of boost. It is now that one gains an appreciation of the power-to-weight ratio of the first generation of monoplane fighters. Although the early Merlins were rated at over 1,000hp, a study of contemporary documents reveals that the 1,030hp is only available at the full throttle altitude of 16,250ft. At sea level the Merlin III produces 890hp, and only 800hp at minimum take-off rpm.

Andy Sephton, Shuttleworth Collection chief pilot

Mk IIC, with four 20mm (0.737in) British Hispano cannon. At first its four-cannon wings were rebuilt from damaged Mk I metal wings.

Mk IID (1943), which had an armament of two 40mm (1.575in) Vickers cannon and two 0.303in guns for aiming purposes, together with additional armour for low-level operations.

Hurricane IIA Z2521, photographed at Langley, was armed with eight 0.303in machine guns and powered by a Merlin XX engine. (via Derek James)

There were four basic versions of the Hurricane II:

Mk IIA (1940), which had Mk I metal wings equipped with eight machine guns.

Mk IIB (1940), with two additional guns in each wing outboard of the landing lights, to make a total armament of twelve 0.303in machine guns, six in each wing. It went into action over occupied France in November 1940.

This Hurricane IIB of No. 2 (RCAF) Squadron is shown carrying two 250lb bombs. Two of the twelve guns normally fitted have been removed. (via M.J.F. Bowyer)

Did You Know?

More than 14,500 Hurricanes were built between 1936 and 1944, including 1,400 in Canada.

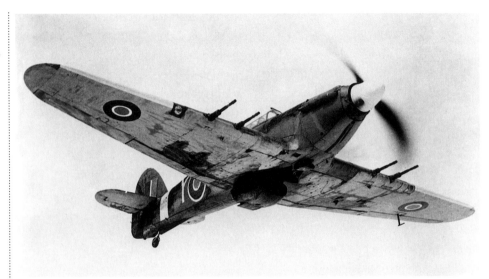

In 1941 both the Mk IIB and IIC were provided with racks under the wings to carry two 250lb (113kg) or 500lb (227kg) bombs. Alternatively, two 45- or 90-gallon fuel tanks could be fitted. Both could be equipped with tropical equipment for service overseas. Development of this fighter-bomber variant resulted in the adoption of the popular name 'Hurri-bomber' for these aircraft.

A Hurricane IIC with 90-gallon long-range ferry tanks fitted under its wings. (via M.J.F. Bowyer)

Subsequent marks of Hurricane were:

Mk III was to have been the British-built Mk II fitted with a 1,300hp (969kW) US-built Packard Merlin 28 engine. It was proposed in late 1941 as insurance against a shortage of Merlin XXs, but was not needed.

Mk IV had a 1,620hp (1,208kW) Rolls-Royce Merlin 24 or 27 engine. It could be

The versatile Mk IV, here with four 20mm cannon, was flown by No. 6 Squadron from 1943 to the end of the war.

➤➤

First flown on 3 April 1943, the prototype Hurricane V, KZ193, was converted from a Mk IV and fitted with a more powerful Merlin 32 driving a four-bladed Rotol propeller. (via M.J.F. Bowyer)

fitted with wings able to carry different armament and loads: two 40mm Vickers cannon and two 0.303in machine guns; eight 3in (7.62cm), 60lb (27kg) rocket projectiles, with three launching rails under each wing, and two 0.303in machine guns; two 250lb or 500lb bombs and two 0.303in machine guns; two 45- or 90-gallon drop tanks and two 0.303in machine guns, with 350lb of additional armour.

> *Close-up of the 40mm Vickers 'S' cannon carried by one of only three Hurricane Vs built. (via M.J.F. Bowyer)*

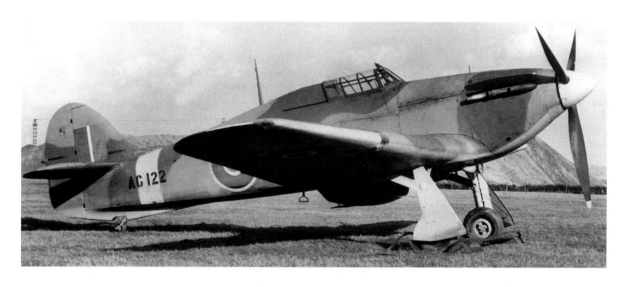

Mk V, initially known as the Mk IIE, had a Rolls-Royce Merlin 27 engine rated at 1,635hp (1,219kW). With this increased take-off power available a four-blade propeller could be fitted. It was otherwise similar to the Mk IV. Only three were built.

Hurricane manufacture was undertaken by the Canadian Car and Foundry Corporation (CCF), with the first aircraft flying on 10 January 1940. A total of 1,391 Hurricanes and Sea Hurricanes was built in Canada in several versions. These included

Originally built by the Canadian Car and Foundry Corporation as a Hurricane I, AG122 was subsequently converted to a Mk II in the UK. (via M.J.F. Bowyer)

➤

*From January 1940, the
Canadian Car and
Foundry Corporation
produced a large number
of Hurricanes, including
this Mk XIIA. (Kev
Baxter)*

the Mk I with Merlin IIIs, Mk X with Packard-built Merlin 28s, Mk XI with Canadian equipment and the Mk XII with Merlin 29s.

The Hurricane Mk X corresponded to the British-built Mk I with a Hamilton Standard Hydromatic propeller, while the Mk XII and XIIA had Packard Merlin 29s developing 1,300hp (969kW).

Although early aircraft were intended to equip Royal Canadian Air Force (RCAF) squadrons at home, most Hurricanes completed by CCF were shipped to England, particularly between March–August 1940.

BIPLANE HURRICANE

One of the more bizarre experimental Hurricanes was the Hillson F.H.40 Slip Wing Hurricane that was briefly tested in 1942–3. Hill and Sons Ltd modified an early Hurricane I (L1884) by fitting a jettisonable top wing. The aim of the biplane project was to give the Hurricane extra lift from the bigger wing area to enable increased fuel to be carried, while maintaining a short take-off run. In turn, this higher take-off weight would give the aircraft substantially more range. After

◄
The Hillson F.H.40 had a second wing mounted above the cockpit to enable the Hurricane to operate from small airfields with a greater load. (via Sue J. Bushell)

Did You Know?

In January 1941 there was a proposal to mount a Hurricane on top of a Consolidated Liberator long-range bomber as a means of providing fighter protection for the bomber on Atlantic patrols.

take-off, the wing would be detached (or slipped) and the Hurricane would carry on normally. The test aircraft was only ever flown as a fixed-wing biplane and the wing-slip was not tried in the air before the project was abandoned.

DIVERSE DUTIES

From early 1941, RAF Hurricane IIAs and IIBs were heavily involved in Fighter Command's offensive sweeps over northern France, when the RAF switched from defensive to offensive operations after the Battle of Britain. Typically, they escorted Bristol Blenheim day bombers of Bomber Command's No. 2 Group, with Spitfires flying top cover. By the end of 1941, Hurricane operations by day over Europe switched to fighter-bomber interdiction sorties. Also in 1941, 'Channel Stop' was flown by Hurricane IIB fighter-bombers of Nos 462 and 607 Squadrons, when Blenheims gave up this hazardous role.

The Hurricane had by now clearly seen its best days as a fighter interceptor, but its excellence as a gun platform held further potential. With the installation of 20mm cannon and, subsequently, rocket projec-tiles, the Hurricane started a new and successful role as a ground-attack fighter.

Black-painted Hurricane IICs became especially adept at night intruder operations over Northern France and the Low Countries and they continued their

Hurricanes painted all-over black continued night operations through 1942. (Andrew P. March)

Carrying the American Eagle on its nose and No. 71 Squadron code XR-T, this Hurricane is painted to represent Z7381, an aircraft flown by the first of the 'Eagle' squadrons, which was formed in October 1940.

Did You Know?

In a five-month period in 1944, No. 6 Squadron's Hurricane IVs, based in Italy and fitted with a drop fuel tank under one wing and rocket projectiles under the other, sank one 5,000-ton ship, 21 schooners, 3 ferries and 11 other ships, in addition to damaging 27 further vessels.

offensive operations well into 1942. Seven Hurricane squadrons took part in the ill-fated Dieppe raid on 14 August 1942.

In the defensive role, some Mk IICs of No. 309 Squadron continued to defend Scotland until as late as October 1944, when they were finally replaced by North American Mustangs.

Rocket-firing Hurricanes, foreshadowing the highly successful role of Hawker

49

Typhoons in 1944, operated from June 1943 until March 1944. They carried eight 3in rocket projectiles, each with a 60lb warhead, delivering a potent punch against ground targets.

After the Battle of Britain, No. 71 Squadron, the celebrated 'Eagle' squadron of volunteer American pilots, was formed and equipped with the Hurricane I. The Mk IID served only with No. 184 Squadron in northern Europe, operating against targets in France and the Low Countries.

A number of retired Mk Is and early IIAs were reintroduced in 1942 for service with the reorganised Air Sea Rescue service. These aircraft retained their armament, being used to search for 'ditched' aircrew and to mount guard over them until the arrival of a rescue launch or Supermarine Walrus amphibian to pick them up.

Before D-Day, 6 June 1944, many Hurricane IICs, albeit under heavy escort by other fighters, carried two 500lb bombs and were used as dive-bombers to attack the heavily defended flying bomb sites in the Pas de Calais area of northern France.

Later in the war, Hurricanes were operated by meteorological reconnaissance 'met' flights. The collection of meteorological data was a twice-daily routine for the RAF at home and abroad (particularly in the Middle East). Such tasks often fell to Hurricane IICs, known as Met IICs.

When the Hurricane came to be replaced in UK-based squadrons, they took on support duties, such as target-towing, army cooperation and anti-aircraft cooperation. However, most of the RAF's Hurricanes had been retired by the end of the war.

HURRICAT

A special Hurricane unit was formed in January 1941 to help protect vital convoys from attacks by enemy long-range maritime bombers. These Hurricanes, mostly converted Mk Is, were equipped to be catapulted from the decks of merchant ships. Each carried two Hurricanes, one mounted on the forecastle catapult ready to go and the other in reserve. The merchant ship had no flight deck; therefore the Hurricane, once shot off, could not return. The SS *Michael E* was the first of these catapult-armed merchant (CAM) vessels. Pilots launching from a CAM ship would have to abandon the aircraft if a shore base could not be reached and parachute into the sea to await rescue. The justification for this hazardous action was that the Hurricane was the only answer to marauding German Focke-Wulf FW 200 Condor four-engined bombers. Flying in a zone extending some 600 miles westward from the French and African coasts, the Luftwaffe had been operating with German U-boats and harrying Allied shipping.

With aircraft carriers, even of the smaller type, at that time at a premium, this was the only means of offering some defence. If the Hurricane could shoot down just one Condor before it attacked a convoy or reported its position to a U-boat, this might help save thousands of tons of shipping and the vital cargoes carried. Coastal Command air patrols had increased their range to a radius of 350 miles from Iceland and Northern Ireland, forcing the U-boats further and further into the mid-Atlantic.

The ultimate decision to launch the Hurricane could be only made by the master of the ship, acting on advice from

Did You Know?
Catapulted from a merchant ship in mid-ocean, seaborne 'Hurricat' pilots had one of the war's most perilous tasks.

▲
Hurricane IA V6756 from the Merchant Ship Fighter Unit, ready to be launched from the bow-mounted catapult of a ship in 1942.

In all, thirty-five ships were fitted with catapults. Some fifty Hurricanes were allocated for the task from Fighter Command in Britain, and a further fifty were earmarked at Halifax, Nova Scotia from Canadian production.

By the beginning of 1943, the odds against the CAM ships were finally acknowledged to be too heavy and hazardous. Of the ships converted with catapult apparatus, eleven had been sunk by enemy action and one more by an accident at sea. By then, a sizeable fleet of merchant aircraft carriers (MACs) had been

the fighter direction officer, the commodore of the convoy, and the senior officer of the escort. On 1 November 1941 a Hurricane was launched from the SS *Empire Foam*, performing the task planned for it. An Fw 200 Condor, which was trying to pick up convoy HX156 in the Atlantic, was driven off, although not shot down.

Extreme priority will be given to fitting out ships to catapult, or otherwise launch, fighter aircraft against German bombers attacking our shipping.

Prime Minister Winston Churchill on 6 March 1941

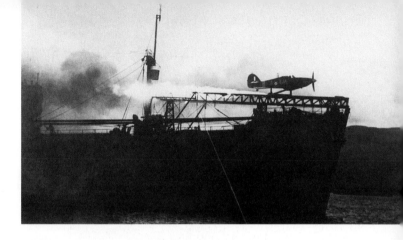

built – ships which could receive their aircraft back on board again. In July 1943 the last of the CAM-ship apparatus was removed and the Hurricanes returned to more normal duties.

In the twenty months of their active service, only eight operational sorties were flown, shooting down five enemy aircraft and seriously damaging two more, for the loss of one Hurricane pilot.

Hurricane being rocket-launched from a CAM ship during trials. The catapult was angled slightly away from the bow line to give the pilot a chance to avoid the path of the ship, should the aircraft have to ditch after launch.

Hitler's forces mounted Operation *Barbarossa*, the invasion of Russia, on 22 June 1941. As a result, Stalin asked for outside help. The UK agreed to supply war materials, and Prime Minister Churchill contracted to ship 200 aircraft a month between October 1941 and June 1942.

During the period of this agreement, nearly 3,000 Hurricanes of all marks went to Russia under Lend-Lease arrangements.

➤

Hurricane production lines at Gloster Aircraft in 1941, many of the completed aircraft being destined for Russia. (via Derek James)

Initially, a small batch of Hurricanes was sent so that the Russians could learn how to assemble and operate the aircraft. In July 1941, forty Hurricanes arrived in Russia to provide assistance and Force *Benedict* was established with 151 Wing. Two squadrons were activated – Nos 81 and 134, with brand new Mk IIAs and IIBs. Their task was to provide some air protection for the ports at which the aircraft would be unloaded. In the far northerly latitude in which they operated, the aircraft's magnetic compasses did not function satisfactorily.

Some crated Hurricanes were despatched by sea to Archangel, where the fighters were assembled. Others were ferried aboard the carrier HMS *Argus* and flown off to an airfield near Murmansk. They then continued on to Afrikanda on

British and Russian pilots discussing technical details about the Hurricane at Murmansk, 1941. (via M.J.F. Bowyer)

Thirty-nine RAF Hurricanes of Nos 81 and 134
Squadrons went to Russia in April 1941. Mk IIB
Z3977 of No. 134 Squadron was photographed at
Vaenga towards the end of the year.
(via Sue J. Bushell)

The Soviet Union received nearly 3,000 Hurricanes
from 1941 under the terms of Lend-Lease, including
this Gloster-built Mk IIB Z5159. (via M.J.F. Bowyer)

the White Sea and to Vaenga, their operating base, escorted by a Russian bomber.

In order to distinguish the squadrons based and operating from Vaenga, unusual markings were applied to the Hurricanes' fuselages. They were uniquely given both letter and number markings to identify individual aircraft to each squadron and their Russian colleagues. At that time Soviet Air Force units used only a numbering system and no letters.

By the autumn of 1941, the weather was deteriorating and the number of patrols and bomber escorts was reduced. With the change in priorities, British crews taught the Russian pilots and ground personnel more about the Hurricane.

In December, having engaged the Luftwaffe with success and familiarised Russian pilots and groundcrew with the aircraft, the RAF contingent returned to the UK. Its aircraft were handed over to the Soviet Northern Fleet Air Force's 72nd Regiment.

Hurricanes represented by far the major part of British aid to Russia during the war. No fewer than 2,952 Hurricanes were despatched, but because of heavy losses suffered by the North Cape convoys, the actual number received in Russia was considerably less.

59

By October 1940, two Hurricane squadrons had become operational in North Africa, having been delivered by sea to Takoradi on the Gold Coast and then flown across the desert to Egypt. In theatre they wore a paint scheme of dark earth, middle stone and azure blue, in the same patterns as UK-based aircraft. Style and presentation of code letters was much more variable. Some aircraft carried a single letter and others none.

In the Middle East it was necessary to equip the Merlin XX engines with sand filters over the carburettor intakes. These

Hurricanes of No. 274 Squadron at Amriya, Egypt in August 1940. The nearest, P2544, was a Gloster-built Mk I. (via Derek James)

A Hurricane Mk I of No. 274 Squadron operating over the desert from Sidi Haneish in 1940. No. 274 was the first unit in Egypt to equip with Hurricanes when the aircraft arrived from East Africa to replace Gladiators. (via Derek James)

▶
A Hurricane I at a desert airstrip practice-firing its guns and creating a sandstorm. Empty bullet cases are falling from under the wings to the ground. (via Derek James)

It is best described as an archaic flying machine. The Hurricane cannot be compared to the P-51 Mustang or P-47 Thunderbolt. It is in a much earlier league of its own, something like a very large and heavy biplane.

USAF pilot

Vokes filters noticeably changed the Hurricane's nose profile and reduced the maximum speed by about 12mph (19km/h), but prolonged engine life. Although the IIC still retained an adequate speed margin over the radial-engined Italian fighters, the appearance of modern German fighters over the Mediterranean in 1941 prompted some squadrons to reduce their armament by removing two outboard guns from their Hurricane IICs to improve their performance. By November 1941, out of 40 British fighter squadrons in the Middle East, 25 flew Hurricanes and, of these, 18 flew Mk IICs.

Throughout the North Africa campaign, the Hurricane played a valuable support role. In the early stages it was the only British monoplane fighter in the area. Versatile and adapted to a wide range of conditions, the reliable Hurricane saw action in many parts of Africa and the Middle East, although squadrons often had to make do with elderly aircraft nearing the end of their service life. During the Desert campaigns of 1941–3, they progressively re-equipped with Mk IIAs, IIBs, IICs and IIDs, Hurricanes eventually serving with twenty-two squadrons. In the period April–May 1941 they fought in the defence of Greece.

Did You Know?
It was said that while the two large cannon of the Mk IID were being fired, the aircraft's speed was reduced by as much as 40mph (64km/h). Against the Afrika Korps in the desert, its reduced speed made it vulnerable to Luftwaffe Messerschmitt Bf 109Fs.

Hawker Hurricane IID.
(via Sue J. Bushell)

From early 1941, No. 2 PRU operated a number of photoreconnaissance Hurricane PR.IIs out of Heliopolis. They were fitted with cameras in the rear fuselage.
(via M.J.F. Bowyer)

From June 1942, the Hurricane IID, equipped with heavy-calibre guns was used as a 'tank-buster' in the Western Desert, and in the Sicilian and Italian campaigns. It was the only operational Allied fighter to be armed with anti-tank guns. With a main armament of two 40mm (1.575in) Vickers cannon, they were used to attack tanks and

other heavily armed vehicles. The two cannon, which fired shells weighing 2.5lb each, were slung under the wings. Above each cannon in the wing, the 0.303in Browning was used chiefly for sighting on a target before the heavy-calibre cannon was fired.

The first operational use of Hurricanes as 'bombers' was when No. 249 Squadron in Malta carried eight 40lb bombs on its aircraft. During the Allied invasion of North Africa during November 1942, following the *Torch* landings in Algeria, Hurricane IICs of No. 43 Squadron were the first Allied fighters to become operational after the capture of Maison Blanche airfield. Sea Hurricane Is and IIBs were deployed on coastal patrols throughout the campaign. The biggest naval action involving Sea Hurricanes was Operation *Pedestal* in August 1942, the build-up of supplies to Malta for the impending advance from El Alamein.

When the Battle of El Alamein commenced on 23 October 1942, there were twenty-five Hurricane squadrons in the Middle East and the number of Mk IID squadrons had increased to four. The tank-busting Hurricanes continued to operate with conspicuous success throughout the remainder of the North Africa campaign. They attacked enemy tanks at very low level from the rear and broke away by turning, rather than climbing, thereby avoiding the anti-aircraft guns to which they were vulnerable. No. 2 PRU operated a number of Hurricane PR.Is and IIs in the reconnaissance role. These were unarmed and capable of operating above 30,000ft (9,144m), and had their normal fuel

◄
No. 6 Squadron, which was to become the last RAF operational squadron to fly the Hurricane, took its Mk IVs across the Adriatic to Yugoslavia in 1945. Seen here is KZ188 at Prkos, loaded with a 44-gallon fuel tank under one wing and four 3in rockets under the other. (via R.L. Ward)

capacity almost trebled by fitting tanks in the gun bays.

The Hurricane saw action in Sicily in July 1943 and then in Italy. No. 208 Squadron in Egypt did much important reconnaissance work operating Hurricane Mk Is with a vertical camera mounted behind the cockpit. Nine Hurricanes serving in North Africa were converted in the field (by 103 Maintenance Unit at Aboukir) for tactical reconnaissance duties from October 1940. These Hurricanes were the first to be painted in desert camouflage. About 200 Hurricane IIAs, Bs and Cs were converted to either armed tactical reconnaissance or unarmed photo reconnaissance aircraft. Hurricane Mk IVs with rocket projectiles arrived in the Mediterranean theatre in time to replace No. 6 Squadron's IIDs for the Tunisian and Sicilian campaigns, thereafter using their 40mm guns to good effect throughout the Battle of Italy. The cast-iron-headed projectiles proved very effective against vehicles, armour, small vessels and structures. The aircraft's new role was to attack Axis shipping and ports on both sides of the Adriatic. No. 6 Squadron adopted the name 'Flying Can Openers' after its exploits. The squadron remained in Italy until the end of the war, and later moved to Palestine, where it became the last Hurricane unit in the RAF before re-equipping with Hawker Tempest Vs on 15 January 1947.

FAR EAST

At the time of the Japanese invasion of Malaya, there were no Hurricanes available to meet the initial assault. From 20 January 1942, the RAF operated fifty-one Hurricanes with Nos 242 and 258 Squadrons at Seletar, Singapore and Nos 232 and 605 in Java and Sumatra. They continued to fly and fight until 7 March 1942. With the fall of Singapore the survivors were withdrawn to Sumatra. Twenty-four more Hurricane Is that were intended for Singapore were diverted to Java, where they were flown by pilots of the Netherlands East Indies Air Force against the Japanese.

Subsequently, during the retreat through Burma, Nos 17, 67 and 135 Squadrons continued the fight from Mingaladon, Akyab and Magwe. During the threatened invasion of Ceylon at Easter 1942,

Hurricane IIBs of Nos 30, 258 and 261 Squadrons fought in the defence of the island's naval base.

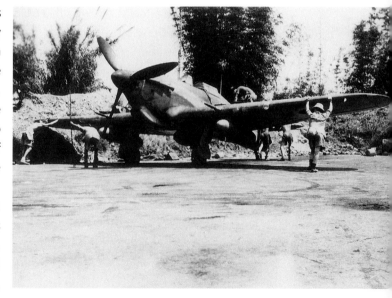

Hurricane Trop TacR Mk IIC of No. 28 Squadron at Imphal in the Indian state of Manipur in 1944. (via R.L. Ward)

69

Hurricane IIDs achieved many successes during the first Burmese Arakan campaign of December 1942, as well as the scattered operations of 1943 which culminated in the second Arakan campaign. By 1944, six squadrons of the Indian Air Force had been equipped with Hurricanes and they participated in the Battles of Kohima and Imphal. As in the Mediterranean, the Mk IV was flown spectacularly in India and Burma. The Allied air forces in Burma and China were primarily engaged in supporting the Army. Tactical and close-air-support were crucial to stopping the Japanese advance.

In preparation for the counter-offensive against the Japanese in Burma, the four squadrons of Mk IIBs and nine of Mk IICs were brought together from India and Ceylon. Eventually, the force comprised no less than twenty-seven Hurricane squadrons. They undertook fighter escort, ground attack and photo and fighter reconnaissance duties. In the final assault on Rangoon in early 1944, the Mk IIDs and IVs decimated Japanese armour, river craft and ground transport. On occasions, the Hurricanes laid smokescreens for attacking B-25 Mitchell bombers. Towards the end of the war, the Hurricane was carrying eight unguided rockets under the wings and, operating from forward strips in Burma, had great success on the Mandalay front. The Hurricane was finally replaced in the Far East Air Force by American Republic P-47 Thunderbolts.

SEA HURRICANE

The Sea Hurricane brought a fighter capability to the Royal Navy's fleet carriers. A conversion of the land-based fighter, it suffered the disadvantage of not being designed specifically for carrier operations. The bulk of Sea Hurricane operations, aboard the carriers *Avenger*, *Eagle*, *Indomitable* and *Victorious*, took place in the Mediterranean theatre.

There were several versions of the Sea Hurricane converted from the Hurricane I, fitted with the Merlin II or III engine.

◄
A pair of Sea Hurricane IBs from 760 Naval Air Squadron. A total of thirty-eight RN FAA squadrons had Sea Hurricanes on strength during the Second World War. (via Sue J. Bushell)

A Sea Hurricane IIB operated by 759 Naval Air Squadron, the Fleet Fighter School at Eastleigh, Nairobi, Kenya. (via Sue J. Bushell)

Appearing in 1941, the Mk IA was fitted with catapult spools, slinging gear and naval radios for use on CAM ships. It was first introduced in the spring of 1941.

The Mk IB had both catapult spools and deck arrester gear for aircraft carrier use, and was the first single-seat carrier fighter monoplane to be used by the Royal Navy.

It went into operation in the Mediterranean in June 1942, particularly distinguishing itself in the defence of Malta convoys that summer. The Sea Hurricane IB provided a more standard naval airpower solution as it was intended to operate from both conventional carriers and the new class of small escort carriers known as MAC (merchant aircraft carrier) ships. These could accommodate twelve Sea Hurricanes and provided protection for convoys in the Atlantic and Mediterranean. Some 260 conversions were undertaken from early 1941, most of them by General Aircraft Ltd (GAL).

Sea Hurricane Mk ICs entered service in January 1942. They had the IB airframe, but with Hurricane IIC four-cannon wings.

The Sea Hurricane Mk II was a conversion of newly built Hurricane IIs (mainly GAL-built), with more powerful Merlin XX engines. They were fitted with a V-frame deck arrester gear and naval radio, but did not have catapult spools. The IIC equipped naval fighter squadrons aboard fleet and escort carriers in most theatres.

Sea Hurricane Mk XIIAs were Canadian-built versions with the Packard Merlin 29 engines. These differed from their British counterparts in having machine-gun rather than cannon armament

Some Hurricane IIs were fitted with arrester hooks in 1943 for use as trainers on dummy decks ashore. Unlike the Sea Hurricane II, they retained standard RAF equipment.

The total number of Sea Hurricane conversions is believed to have been about 800, of which the Royal Navy had taken delivery of 600 by mid-1942. Most front-line units changed to newer types during 1943. Thirty-eight Fleet Air Arm squadrons operated Sea Hurricanes, the last being 842 Squadron, which relinquished its aircraft in April 1944. The Squadron's final operation was from HMS *Striker*, providing cover for the carrier's Fairey Swordfish torpedo bombers as they attacked German shipping along the Norwegian coast.

FOREIGN DELIVERIES

Pre-war deliveries of Hurricane Is to overseas air arms included Turkey (15), Romania (12), and one each to Poland and Persia. Twelve went to Finland after that country was attacked by Russia in 1939 and were flown in the Winter and Continuation Wars with some success.

Twenty-four Mk Is were delivered to Yugoslavia from 1938, and a further 100 were to have been built by Zmaj (60) and Rogozarski (40), although in the event only 20 were completed by the former.

Belgium acquired a manufacturing licence for the Mk I in addition to purchasing twenty (of which fifteen were delivered) from the UK. Eighty were ordered from the Belgian company Avions Fairey, of which only three were completed by the time Belgium capitulated. The Belgian aircraft differed from the RAF's in having provision for two 0.5in and two 7.7mm machine guns as an alternative to the eight Brownings.

Following France's surrender to Germany in June 1940, numerous Free French pilots

One of the Hurricane IICs that was supplied to Persia (now Iran). (via Derek James)

Hurricane IIC HV608, supplied to Turkey from the RAF Middle East Air Force in 1942. (via R.L. Ward)

and groundcrew joined the Allies and eventually formed several Free French units, flying alongside the RAF and USAAF in Syria, Libya and Algeria.

Turkey ordered fifteen new production Hurricane Is, which were delivered in the autumn of 1940. Further small supplies of Mk IIBs and IICs were supplied as part of an aid programme in 1942. The machines supplied to Turkey had Vokes tropical filters fitted.

The Irish Air Corps (IAC) acquired a Hurricane which had force-landed in 1942. Two further were acquired by the same means and in 1943 four ex-RAF Mk Is were supplied direct. Towards the end of the war, the Air Ministry released twelve Hurricane IIBs and IICs for service with the IAC, these being operated from Baldonnel between 1944 and 1947.

South Africa received six Mk Is from RAF stocks early in 1939. A further twenty-four were supplied at the outbreak of war, these going to Kenya and Sudan to counter the threat posed by the Italians in Abyssinia. Five South African squadrons saw action in North Africa from 1940 to 1944.

The Royal Australian Air Force (RAAF) made limited used of the Hurricane, three squadrons operating the type in the Middle East under RAF control. Only one Hurricane (Mk I V7476) was taken on RAAF strength 'at home'. It was allocated RAAF serial A60-1, but wore the British identity.

The Egyptian Air Force, manned principally by Egyptian pilots flying with the Desert Air Force in defence of home bases, received twenty Mk IIBs and IICs from RAF stock from 1941. They remained in service for the rest of the war. The only other air force to receive Hurricanes during the war was India. From 1941, some 300 Mk IIBs, IICs, IIDs, IVs and XIIs were delivered. In addition a small number were equipped for tactical reconnaissance.

Advances in RAF aircraft during 1939–45 were due not so much to changes in basic design philosophy as to progressive increases in the power of engines, together with constant improvements in operational techniques. However, by 1945, piston-engined fighters had reached the limit of their development. The first squadron of Gloster Meteor jet fighters had been in action since the summer of 1944 and the de Havilland Vampire was coming into service.

With the war over, the RAF dwindled rapidly and the majority of aircraft that had been in service instantly became surplus to requirements. Most were flown to Maintenance Units, where they were stored until they could be scrapped. By the end of 1946, Fighter Command possessed no more than 192 front-line aircraft in eighteen day and six night fighter squadrons – all reduced to a cadre of eight aircraft per squadron, without reserves. The Hurricane did not feature in this list, and its Hawker piston-engined successors, the Typhoon and Tempest, were serving only overseas in Germany, the Middle East and Aden. This decline in numbers was not reversed until the Berlin blockade crisis of 1948–9.

Soon after the end of the war, trouble brewed up in Palestine. No. 6 Squadron with its Hurricanes was used mainly to search for illegal Jewish immigrants infiltrating into Palestine by sea. It was the last RAF unit to fly Hurricanes.

In 1946 the Persian contract, which had been in abeyance since 1939, was re-opened, with ex-RAF machines being delivered. Over forty IICs were sold to

Hawker took a proven construction from its biplanes and produced a low technology monoplane fighter. A very safe and reliable aircraft with a good rate of climb.

Stephen Grey, The Fighter Collection

Portugal during 1946–7 (having been returned to Hawkers from the RAF in 1945). These were chosen from the large stock of surplus late-series IICs.

The Battle of Britain Memorial Flight (BBMF) was formed at Biggin Hill, initially as the Historic Aircraft Flight, on 11 July 1957. At this time, it had four Spitfires and a Hurricane (LF363) on strength. In 1958 the flight moved first to North Weald, then Martlesham Heath. It moved again to Horsham St Faith in 1960 and to RAF Coltishall in 1964. After that date, the flight gradually increased in size, with further Spitfires and, in 1972, a second Hurricane, PZ865, the last of the type built. It was

BBMF Hurricane LF363 was painted for its early years to represent the No. 242 Squadron aircraft flown by its CO, Douglas Bader, in the Battle of Britain.

presented to the Flight by Hawker Siddeley in March 1972. In March 1976 the BBMF moved to RAF Coningsby, Lincolnshire, its present home, where it has five Spitfires, two Hurricanes, a Lancaster, a Dakota and the last two operational Chipmunks used for training.

Hurricane IIC LF363 is believed to be the last Hurricane to enter service with the RAF. It first flew on 1 January 1944, was delivered to 5 MU four weeks later and was in continuous RAF service from then until a crash-landing in 1991. The aircraft served with Nos 63, 309 (Polish) and 26 Squadrons before the end of the war. Unlike many other Hurricanes, LF363 was not scrapped but served on various station flights and appeared in the movie *Angels One-Five*. In 1949 it was the personal mount of Air Vice-Marshal S.F. Vincent. It was refurbished by Hawkers over the winter 1952/3. In 1954, whilst operated by the RAF Waterbeach Station Flight, it appeared in the television series *The War in the Air*. The following year, it featured in the film *Reach for the Sky* (Gp Capt Douglas Bader's life-story) and the 1968 film *Battle of Britain*. It became part of the RAF Historic Flight at Biggin Hill in July 1957.

On 11 September 1991, whilst flying from RAF Coningsby to participate in a Battle of Britain air display in Jersey, the aircraft's engine started running rough, and smoke came from all twelve exhaust stubs. The pilot attempted to land at RAF Wittering but the engine failed completely, resulting in a crash-landing, after which the Hurricane was seriously damaged by an extensive fire. LF363 was rebuilt (paid for by the sale of one of the BBMF's Spitfires) during a four-year restoration from 1994 to 1998 by Historic Flying Ltd (HFL) at Audley End. It was airborne for the first time in September 1998 and returned to the BBMF before the end of the month.

LF363 was painted in the markings of a No. 56 Squadron Hurricane, coded US-C, until it had a major service over the winter

➤
Following its crash landing at RAF Wittering in September 1991, LF363 was badly burnt. It is shown here at Coningsby before full restoration commenced. (Brian Strickland)

➤➤
After its rebuild, LF363 was first painted in No. 56 Squadron colours.

The last Hurricane built, PZ865 was rolled out at Langley, Bucks in July 1944, making its first flight on the 27th. (via Derek James)

of 2005–6. It reappeared for the 2006 display season in the colour scheme of Hurricane I P3878, YB-W. This was the aircraft that Flg Off (later Air Vice-Marshal CBE, DSO, DFC, AFC and bar) Harold Bird-Wilson flew with No. 17 Squadron from Tangmere and Debden during the Battle of Britain.

PZ865, the last Hurricane ever built, rolled off the production line at Hawker's factory at Langley, Bucks in the summer of 1944. It carried the inscription 'The Last of the Many' on its port and starboard fuselage sides. The aircraft was almost immediately purchased back from the Air Ministry by Hawkers and initially moth-balled, before being employed as a company communication and test aircraft. In 1959, wearing the civil registration G-AMAU and painted in royal blue with a gold trim, it was entered in the King's Cup Air Race by HRH Princess Margaret. Flown by Gp Capt Peter Townsend, it achieved second place.

During the 1960s, PZ865 was returned to its wartime camouflage scheme and was used as a company 'hack' and as chase plane on the development flights involving the P.1127 Kestrel, the forerunner of the Harrier. It appeared in the films *Angels One-Five* and *Battle of Britain* and also made numerous display appearances, often in the hands of the famous Hawker test pilot Bill Bedford.

In late 1971, PZ865 was given a complete overhaul and in the following March it was flown to RAF Coltishall to be donated by Hawker Siddeley to the Battle of Britain Memorial Flight. In recent years, the aircraft has carried the desert markings

of No. 261 Squadron, representing one of the first twelve Hurricanes to be delivered to Malta. Following major servicing at RAF St Athan over the winter of 1998, it was painted in the colours of No. 5 Squadron, coded 'Q', from its time in South East Asia Command. In 2007 it was painted to represent Hurricane IIC BE581, JX-E, *Night Reaper*, the aircraft flown by the Czech pilot ace Flt Lt Karel 'Kut' Kuttelwascher, DFC* during night intruder operations with No. 1(F) Squadron from Tangmere in 1942. The single-seat Hurricanes were not radar-equipped, so targets could only be found visually and without the benefits of modern aids to night vision.

JX-E wore the Night Reaper motif on the starboard engine cowling and 'Kut' had swastika symbols painted under the cockpit side. When his three kills from the night of 5 May 1942 were added there were eleven swastikas displayed ('Kut' eventually achieved a total of eighteen confirmed kills). The aircraft's rudder and a panel on the port wing had to be replaced with black-painted items from a 'Turbinlite' Hurricane (BD770) because of flak damage incurred by BE581 on that sortie. This is all faithfully replicated on PZ865 as a 'snap-shot in time'.

A new set of hand-formed flame-damper exhaust stubs (originally developed for day and night operations) were fitted to PZ865 in September 2006 so that the aircraft could be returned to its configuration when it came off the production line at Langley.

The Hurricane is just a big pussy cat.

Pete Thorn, Hurricane pilot with the RAF Memorial Flight (later the BBMF)

◀

Among the paint schemes carried by PZ865 after it joined the BBMF in March 1971 were the desert markings of No. 261 Squadron.

Did You Know?

The 12,780th and final Hurricane built in England, a Mk IIC, was completed at Hawker's Langley factory in July 1944. This aircraft (PZ865) is still flying with the RAF Battle of Britain Memorial Flight.

The last Hurricane ever built, PZ865 was purchased by the manufacturer and did not join the BBMF until March 1971.

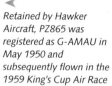

Retained by Hawker Aircraft, PZ865 was registered as G-AMAU in May 1950 and subsequently flown in the 1959 King's Cup Air Race at Coventry.

More recently, PZ865 has appeared in South East Asia Command colours, coded Q of No. 5 Squadron while the squadron was at Assam in late 1943.

After overhaul by ARC at Duxford in 2005, PZ865 was repainted to represent Hurricane IIC of No. 1(F) Squadron BE581, coded JX-E.

Built as a Mk XIIA RCAF 5589, this Hurricane was newly painted in 2007 to represent Mk IIB BD707 flown by No 402 Squadron, RCAF, in September 1941. (Darren Harbar)

HURRICANE SURVIVORS

At the end of 2006 there were over forty surviving Hurricanes, of which fourteen were in airworthy condition – six in the UK including the BBMF's pair. There were two Sea Hurricanes, one in the USA and the other with the Shuttleworth Collection at Old Warden. Over the next few years a further nine Hurricanes are likely to be made airworthy, including six with Hawker Restorations at Milden,

◄

Historic Aircraft Collection's Canadian-built Hurricane XIIA 25140. (Gary Brown)

Death Warmed Up *nose art on Malta Aviation Museum's Z3055, representing HA-E of No. 126 Squadron.*

at the Malta Aviation Museum is typical of the meticulous rebuilds currently being undertaken around the world. Powered by a Merlin XX engine, Z3055 was delivered to the RAF on 27 February 1941. After storage, it was shipped to Malta, flying off HMS *Ark Royal* on 6 June 1941 during Operation *Rocket*. It flew with No. 46 Squadron, later changing to No. 126 Squadron at Safi. The Hurricane was subsequently lost in the sea off Malta in an unrecorded accident that killed the pilot. Discovered on the seabed off the Blue Grotto, Z3055 was salvaged on 19 September 1995. With a number of key donations, it is being returned to taxiable condition by David Polidano and museum volunteers. It has been painted to represent HA-E of No. 126 Squadron, with *Death Warmed Up* nose art as shown in an original wartime photograph.

Suffolk. Many of the aircraft now available for rebuild have been recovered from Russia. The majority of the Hurricanes preserved in the USA are Canadian-built Mk XIIs that were flown by the RCAF in Canada.

Although it is not being restored to fly, the Hurricane IIA is undergoing restoration

There is just one airworthy Hurricane I that actually took part in the Battle of Britain – Peter Vacher's R4118. Delivered new to No. 605 (County of Warwick) Squadron, RAuxAF, in August 1940, it flew forty-nine combat sorties during the Battle

◄

The cockpit of Hurricane IIA Z3055 restored to original configuration at the Malta Aviation Museum.

of Britain, during which it accounted for five German aircraft. It was damaged in a dogfight on 22 October 1940. After rebuild, it flew with No. 111 Squadron from February 1941, before being relegated to training duties. At the end of 1943, R4118 was shipped to India, where it remained in a crate until 1947. Donated to Banaras University, it stood in a compound for nearly fifty years before Peter Vacher managed to get permission to bring it to the UK. Very carefully restored to its 1940 condition by Hawker Restorations at Milden, Suffolk, R4118 was flown again on 23 December 2004. Painted in No. 605 Squadron colours with its original code letters UP-W, it is a fitting tribute to Sydney Camm's distinguished fighter that did so much to stem the aerial attacks on Britain and in service around the world.

◄
Peter Vacher's R4118, the only surviving Hurricane I that actually flew in the Battle of Britain, has been flying since December 2004. (Darren Harbar)

During the rebuild of R4118, we discovered that major components like ailerons, elevators and rudder were built at different times by different companies over a six year period, yet the standard of engineering was such that overhauled components interchanged with old damaged ones with no special fitting. R4118, a Gloster-built airframe, is fitted with Canadian-built wings, rebuilt after accident damage by the London, Midland and Scottish Railway Company at Derby.

Peter Vacher, owner of restored Hurricane I R4118

PRESERVED HURRICANES

The following substantially complete Hurricanes and Sea Hurricanes are preserved, airworthy (marked *) or under active restoration (marked #).

L1592	I	Science Museum, London.
L1639#	I	Cambridge Bomber and Fighter Society, Little Gransden.
P2617	I	RAF Museum, Hendon.
P2902 (G-ROBT)#	I	Hawker Restorations, Milden, Suffolk.
P2970 (N678DP)*	XII	Ed Russell, Ontario, Canada.
P3311#	I	Warbird Recovery, Fort Collins, Colorado, USA.
P3554# (composite)	I	Air Defence Collection, Salisbury, Wilts.
P3351 (ZK-TPK)*	I	Privately owned, Christchurch, New Zealand.
P3717 (DR348)#	I	Hawker Restorations, Milden, Suffolk.
P3395 (KX829)	IV	Millennium Discovery Centre, Birmingham.
R4118 (G-HUPW)*	I	Peter Vacher, Oxford.
V7497 (G-HRLI)	I	Hawker Restorations, Milden, Suffolk.
Z2315	IIB	Imperial War Museum, Duxford, Cambs.
Z2389#	IIA	Brooklands Museum, Weybridge, Surrey.
Z3055#	IIA	Malta Aviation Museum, Ta' Qali, Malta.
Z3174	IIA	National Museum of the USA, Dayton, Ohio, USA.
Z5140 (G-HURI)*	XIIA	Historic Aircraft Collection, Duxford.

➤

Photographed flying from Phoenix, Arizona in October 1995, Hurricane XII P2970 is now with Ed Russell in Canada. (Adam Smith)

Hurricane I P3351 has been airworthy at Wanaka, New Zealand since January 2000. (Brian Strickland)

◄
Originally built in 1942 in Canada, Hurricane XIIA 5711/Z5140 was acquired by the Historic Aircraft Collection at Duxford in 2002.

On static display at Old Warden from 1961, Sea Hurricane IB Z7015 was slowly restored to fly at Staverton and Duxford from 1975, making its first flight on 16 September 1995. (Darren Harbar)

Restored by Hawker Restorations, the former converted Sea Hurricane AE977 was rebuilt as a Mk X and flown at Wattisham on 7 June 2000. It is now with the Planes of Fame at Chino, California.

Z5252 (G-BWHA)	IIB	Hawker Restorations, Milden, Suffolk.
Z5207 (G-BYDL)#	IIB	Retro Track and Air (UK), Dursley, Glos.
Z7015 (G-BKTH)*	Sea IB	Shuttleworth Collection, Old Warden.
AB832	IIB	Air Force Museum, Palam AFB, New Delhi, India.
AE977 (N33TF)*	X	Cinema Air, Chino, California, USA.
BD707 (G-HURR)*	XIIB	Spitfire Limited, Duxford.
BN230	IIC	RAF Manston Memorial Pavilion.

KZ321 (G-HURY)*	IV	Vintage Wings of Canada, Gatineau, Ottawa, Canada.
LD619 (5285)	IIC	SAAF National Museum, Johannesburg, South Africa.
LF363*	IIC	RAF, Battle of Britain Memorial Flight, Coningsby, Lincs.
LF345 (LF658)	IIC	Musée Royal de l'Armée, Brussels, Belgium.

➤

Operated by Spitfire Ltd at Duxford, Hurricane XIIB BD707 is here being flown by John Romain in May 2007. (Darren Harbar)

➤➤

Hurricane IV KZ321 was restored and flown by The Fighter Collection at Duxford before being sold to Vintage Wings of Canada in 2006.

Peter Teichman's Hurricane 5403 on rebuild at Hawker Restorations Ltd in May 2007.

First flown at Wattisham on 15 March 2006, Hurricane XIIA BW881 is now painted as RCAF 5429 with the Flying Heritage Collection in Seattle. (Kev Baxter)

LF686	IIC	National Air and Space Museum, Washington DC, USA.
LF738	IIC	RAF Museum, Cosford.
PZ865 (G-AMAU)*	IIC	RAF, Battle of Britain Memorial Flight, Coningsby, Lincs.
CCF-96 (N96RW)*	XII	Lone Star Flight Museum, Galveston, Texas, USA.
RCAF 5389	XII	Aerospace Museum, Calgary, Canada.
RCAF 5403 (G-HRLO)	X	Peter Teichman, Milden, Suffolk.
RCAF 5418	XII	Reynolds Aviation Museum, Alberta, Canada.
RCAF 5429 (BW881)*	XIIA	Flying Heritage Collection, Seattle, Washington, USA.
RCAF 5447 (C-GGAJ)#	XII	Vintage Wings of Canada, Gatineau, Ottawa, Canada.
RCAF 5450 (G-TDTW)	XII	Hawker Restorations, Milden, Suffolk.
RCAF 5487 (G-CBOE)#	IIB	Peter Tuplin, Thruxton.
RCAF 5584	XII	National Aeronautical Collection, Ontario, Canada.
RCAF 5625#	IIC	Moore Aviation Restoration, Toronto, Canada.
RCAF 5667 (N943HH)#	XIIB	The Fighter Factory, Virginia Beach, Virginia, USA.
HC-452 (ex N2394)	I	Tikkakoski Finnish Air Force Museum, Finland.
9539	IV	Muzej J.V, Beograd-Zemun, Serbia and Montenegro.

APPENDIX I – SPECIFICATIONS

HURRICANE IA

Engine:	Rolls-Royce Merlin II or III liquid-cooled V12 piston engine, with single-speed/ single-stage supercharger
Power:	1,030hp (768kW)
Max speed:	324mph (521km/h)
Length:	31ft 5in (9.58m)
Wingspan:	40ft 0in (12.19m)
Height:	13ft 1in (3.95m)
Armament:	8 x Browning 0.303in machine guns
Max all-up weight:	6,661lb (3,021kg)
Range:	440 miles (708km)
Entered service:	1937

HURRICANE II

Engine:	Rolls-Royce Merlin XX or 22
Power:	1,289hp/1,460hp (961kW/1,089kW)
Max speed:	336mph (568km/h)
Length:	32ft 3in (9.83m)
Wingspan:	40ft 0in (12.19m)
Height:	13ft 3in (4.04m)
Armament:	IIA – 8 x 0.303in machine guns IIB – 6/8/12 x 0.303in machine-guns IIC – 4 x 20mm cannon IID – 2 x 40mm cannon and 2 x 0.303in machine guns
Max all-up weight:	7,670lb (3,478kg)
Range:	920 miles (1,480km) with two drop-tanks
Entered service:	IIA – 1940; IIB –1940; IIC –1941; IID – 1943

HURRICANE IV

Engine:	Rolls-Royce Merlin 24 or 27 with two-speed/single-stage supercharger
Power:	1,620hp (1,208kW)
Max speed:	330mph (531km/h)
Length:	32ft 3in (9.83m)
Wingspan:	40ft 0in (12.19m)
Height:	13ft 3in (4.04m)
Armament:	2 x 0.303in machine guns and 4 x 20mm/2 x 40mm cannon or 8 x rocket projectiles or 2 x 250lb or 500lb bombs or 2 x 45- or 90-gallon drop-tanks
Max all-up weight:	8,463lb (3,838kg)
Range:	495 miles (790km)
Entered service:	1943

Hurricane IV KZ321.

1934 **May:** The first drawings, for the fuselage and engine mountings, of the 'Interceptor Fury Monoplane' reached Hawker's Experimental Section at Kingston.

1934 **4 September:** Sydney Camm's latest plans for his new monoplane were submitted to the Air Ministry, based upon a formula designed to deliver 310mph (498km/h) at 15,000ft.

1935 **21 February:** First prototype, K5083, officially ordered as the High Speed Monoplane to the design submitted in September 1934.

1935 **6 November:** Maiden flight of K5083, powered by a Rolls-Royce 'C' engine, with Hawker's chief test pilot, P.W.S. 'George' Bulman, at the controls. It had a strut-braced tailplane and lightly framed canopy. A retractable tailwheel was a feature unique to the prototype.

1936 **7 February:** Service trials of K5083 commenced at RAF Martlesham Heath.

1936 **1 June:** 600 Hurricanes ordered by the Air Ministry.

1936 **27 June:** The name 'Hurricane' officially adopted.

1936 **20 July:** Specification 15/36 agreed for the production Hurricane I, with a Merlin II engine.

1937 **September:** Gloster Aircraft awarded a direct contract, initially to build 500 Hurricanes.

1937 **12 October:** Maiden flight of the first production Hurricane I, L1547.

1937   **15 December:** L1548 joined No. 111 Squadron at RAF Northolt, the first monoplane fighter to enter RAF front-line service. A further two were delivered by the end of the year.

1938   **January:** A ventral fin fairing was added beneath the rear fuselage to assist spin recovery.

1938   **February:** Sqn Ldr John Gillman, CO of No. 111 Squadron flew a Hurricane from Edinburgh to London at an average speed of 408mph (523km/h). The flight was aided by a strong tailwind, the true speed being 325mph at 17,000ft.

1938   **March:** No. 3 Squadron at RAF Kenley received Hurricanes to replace Gloster Gladiators.

1938   **29 August:** Trials commenced with L1562 fitted with a three-bladed DH two-pitch propeller.

1938   **November:** 1,000 further Hurricanes ordered.

1938   **31 December:** 195 Hurricanes were flying with RAF squadrons.

1939   **4 January:** A Hurricane production order placed with the Canadian Car and Foundry Company at Fort William, Canada. The first of these arrived in England in June 1940.

1939   **24 January:** First flight of Hurricane G-AFKX, a Hawker development aircraft fitted with a Merlin III engine to try to improve the performance. It reached a speed of 344mph (554km/h) at 15,000ft – the fastest Hurricane at that time.

1939 28 April: The first flight of Hurricane L1877 fitted with metal stressed-skin wings.

1939 17 May: Hurricane I L1669 fitted with a tropical filter flown for the first time.

1939 24 May: Hurricane L1750 flown with underslung 20mm cannon.

1939 3 September: Outbreak of Second World War. By this date, 475 Hurricanes had been delivered (at a cost of about £5,000 each). Sixteen squadrons and two half-squadrons were equipped with Hurricanes.

1939 20 October: First flight of a Gloster-built Mk I. First deliveries from Hucclecote, Glos were made in December.

1939 30 October: The first enemy aircraft, a Dornier Do 17, was shot down on the Western Front over Toul, by Hurricane L1842 of No. 85 Squadron.

1940 10 January: First flight of a Canadian-built Hurricane (P5170).

1940 7 May: Hurricane P3462 was flown with two fixed 44-gallon long-range fuel tanks.

1940 25 May: Hurricane's first flight from the deck of a carrier, HMS *Glorious*.

1940 11 June: The first Mk II (P3269) powered by a 1,289hp Merlin XX with a Rotol constant-speed propeller made its maiden flight.

1940 2 August: Hurricanes of No. 261 Squadron were flown off the carrier HMS *Argus* to relieve the land-based Gloster Sea Gladiators in the defence of Malta.

1940 **7 August:** By this date, the RAF had received 2,309 Hurricanes, compared with 1,400 Spitfires.

1940 **13 August:** First night victory of the war outside western Europe, when a Hurricane operating from Malta engaged an Italian S.79.

1940 **4 September**: The first production eight-gun Mk II Series 1 was delivered to No. 111 Squadron at RAF Croydon.

1940 **10 September:** Hurricanes shot down an Italian bomber over the Western Desert for the first time.

1940 **September:** From this month, all new Hurricanes leaving the Langley factory were Mk IIs.

1940 **11 November:** First notable combat after the Battle of Britain when Hurricanes shot down eleven Italian aircraft (their first and only raid on Britain) without loss.

1941 **20 January:** Official approval given for Hawker to proceed with 100 sets of wings with four Hispano cannon.

1941 **19 February:** Hurricanes of No. 33 Squadron deployed to Eleusis in Greece to counter increased pressure by the Italians and the threat of Germany invading the Balkans.

1941 **February:** First deliveries of Mk IIB (with twelve guns) to No. 56 Squadron at RAF North Weald.

1941 **6 April:** The German invasion of the Balkans. In defence, the Yugoslav Air Force had thirty-eight

Hurricanes, but these remained in action for only a week.

1941 **April:** The standard Mk IIC, with four cannon, introduced into service on Nos 1 and 3 Squadrons.

1941 **May:** The Brooklands factory, which had built 2,815 Hurricanes, closed and replaced by the purpose-built factory and airfield at Parlaunt Park Farm at Langley, Bucks. Brooklands was handed over to Vickers Aircraft.

1941 **1 June:** Thirty Hurricane Is and IIs formed 71(ME) OTU at Ismailia, Egypt to train new Hurricane pilots.

1941 **3 August:** First enemy aircraft destroyed by a Sea Hurricane IA that had been catapulted from a ship.

1941 **7 September:** The first twenty-four new Hurricane IIBs for Russia took off for Archangel from the escort carrier HMS *Argus*.

1941 **11 September:** Hurricanes of Nos 81 and 134 Squadrons, 151 Wing, began operations from Vaenga, near Murmansk in Northern Russia.

1941 **20 October:** The first 'Hurri-bombers' – Hurricane IIBs fitted with bomb racks – went into action against Italian airfields from Hal Far, Malta.

1941 **26 October:** Russian pilots flying Hurricanes made their first kill, a Luftwaffe Messerschmitt Bf 110.

1941 **1 November:** First operational flight by a Canadian Hurricane IIB fighter-bomber.

1941 **November:** The first Soviet-built Hurricane shot down a Ju 88.

1941 **December:** Prototype Mk IID (Z2326) made its maiden flight.

1942 **21 March:** Last of 2,750 Gloster-built Hurricanes was delivered to the RAF.

1942 **June:** The first Mk IICs in the Far East were delivered to No. 607 Squadron.

1942 **19 August:** Dieppe landings, in which many Hurricane squadrons were involved.

1943 **14 March:** Prototype Mk IIE (later known as Mk V) first flown.

1943 **March:** First Mk IV (KX405) made its maiden flight.

1943 **June:** Hurricane IIBs and IICs were being flown by sixteen squadrons in India, Burma and Ceylon.

1944 **September:** The last new-build Hurricane, a IIC (PZ865), left the production line at Langley.

1945 **9 April:** No. 6 Squadron moved to Prkos in Yugoslavia and remained until the end of the war in Europe.

1946 **27 September:** A Persian Air Force two-seat Hurricane, 2-31 (ex-K2232), was flown.

1947 **January:** The last Hurricanes in RAF service, Mk IVs with No. 6 Squadron, were retired.

1952 **September:** Hurricane IIC LF363 arrived at Hawkers for refurbishment before returning to the RAF.

1960 The last Hurricane was used as an observation 'chase plane' during the flight trials of Hawkers' Kestrel V/STOL prototype.

1972 **March:** Hurricane PZ865 was flown to RAF Coltishall and presented to the BBMF by Hawkers.

1991 **11 September:** BBMF Hurricane IIC LF363 crash-landed at RAF Wittering and was badly damaged..

1995 **16 September:** The world's first restored Sea Hurricane IB (Z7015), powered by a Merlin III, was flown at Duxford.

1998 **September:** A seven-year rebuild of LF363 was completed and it returned to the BBMF.

2004 **23 December:** Recovered from India by Peter Vacher, the Battle of Britain veteran Hurricane I R4118 flew again for the first time in over sixty years at Cambridge.

◄ *Sea Hurricane IB Z7015.*

Total Hurricane production is generally quoted as 14,533. Breakdown by individual marks is difficult to ascertain accurately as many were conversions. It should be noted that no Sea Hurricanes were built as such – they were all conversions.

Prototype	1	Mk IV	2,000
Mk I	3,719	Mk V	3
Canadian Mk I	600	Canadian Mk IIB	20
Mk IIA	451	Canadian Mk X	446
Mk IIB	2,048	Canadian Mk XI	200
Mk IIC	3,400	Canadian Mk XII	398
Mk IID	800		

➤

The Hawker production line at Langley in early 1944.